Celebrating one year of publishing great connections

MY CONNECTIONS MAGAZINE

Connections

MAGAZINE

April Showers

MaY FLOWeRS

SiDeWaLK CHaLK

Blowing bubbles

Mud Puddles

RIDING BIKES

7 Belly Fat Burning Foods

CONNECTIONS MAGAZINE SPRING 2014

More inside tips, facts, and practical experience result.

Sponsored: HAPPY BIRTHDAY "My Connections Magazine".

Wordpress   Google Adsense Direct   Med Malpractice Insurance   deleonpost.com
Police Without Borders We Connect 2 Publishing and Digital Network News U.S. Journal

Feature Story Inside

All publishing and contact information available at myconnectionsmagazine.com By Eddieadel & associates

Table of Contents:

On the Cover Spring Showers. First day of Spring March 21. It is not so anymore. Global warming have frustrated the weather and climate forecast. We are in what suppose to be almost summer, but yet to come. It is spring all over California. The Southland enjoying the cold temperature at night, and warm afternoon with little Santa Ana wind for the most part of the mid day about 11 AM until 2 PM.

The feature story is almost our twin story. As My Connections Magazine turn one year old the struggle continue of making this publication successful. Success to us is measured by the quality of work. We feel that we are always second to best of the best in our search for best content, perfect picture, and meeting all of our readers demands. Yours truly, the editing team.

Spring 2014 Fashion statement- MY FASHION CONNECTIONS

Think of it as power dressing with a sense of humor. Pinstripes were taken for a playful spin at the round of fashion shows just ended. The young woman on the left calls to mind a "Blond Ambition"-era Madonna in her double-breasted bustier top and matching pants, which she wore with cold-weather layers and lighthearted accessories. The model and blogger Zanata Morginwore wide-leg Acne pinstripe pants, with a dark coat and sneakers; the front-row fixture   Miroslava Duma was coolly chic in a Salvatore Ferragamo pinstripe suit and a bustier top; and the stylist Ece Sukan wore a pinstripe suit with a turtleneck, the skirt slit up to there. This is a trend just about any woman can embrace. Dig into your wardrobe or invest in new pinstripes, like the smart Acne suit at right — and have a little fun.

You can always style your pinstripes more soberly for business hours. NY Times

Spring Fashion That Makes a Statement

My Diet Connections:

Cover: Belly Fat Burning Foods

A bloated stomach not only hampers your personality but also makes you uncomfortable. We share a list of food that aids in getting a flat stomach.

1-Almonds: This tiny food is not only rich in skin-boosting vitamin E and protein, but their richness in fibre content helps you to stay full for a longer duration. Even though they are slightly high in calories but that will not contribute to belly fat, so keep swapping a handful of almonds as snacks to curb your hunger.

2-Apples: Apples are packed with fibre, which makes your belly feel full. Thus, avoiding over eating; besides it also fills your body with maximum nutrients.

3-Avocado: This is a truly magic fruit, due to their richness in various vital nutrients. Avocado is rich in fibre, which helps to keep hunger at bay and the presence of monounsaturated fatty acids helps to burn belly fat easily.

4-**Cucumber:** Cucumber is an extremely refreshing and low-calorie food. They contain approximately 96 percent water content, which makes it a cooling food. One full cucumber contains just 45 calories, making it sexy stomach food.

5-**Green leafy vegetable:** Want to get a flat tummy instantly? Then fill for plate with green leafy vegetables. All types of green leafy vegetables are extremely low in calories, full of fibre and offer several vital vitamins and minerals that help to ease water retention without causing the bloating and tummy discomfort.

6-**Beans:** Consuming means on a regular basis helps to get rid of the body fat, develop body muscles and improves digestion. Beans also help to feel full for a longer duration, thus avoiding over indulgence. Add beans to your diet, if you want your middle to be sexy and firm.

7-**Watermelon:** The name says it all - this giant fruit contains 82 percent water, which helps to keep you full for a longer duration and also removes excess sodium present in the body. This super sweet fruit, is also rich in vitamin C and contains barely 100 calories in one cup. So start eating this delicious fruit as a snack, if you wish to have a body like your favourite celeb.

Lower Abs best select exercises

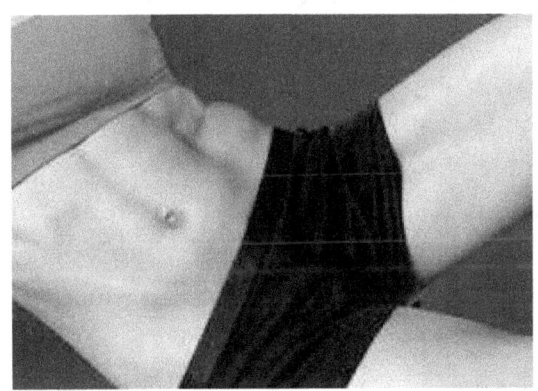

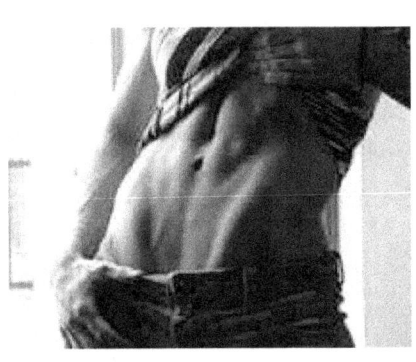

10 Simple Steps to Enhance Detoxification.

Proper detoxification is so essential for health that you need to start enhancing your body's ability to detoxify today. Here is how to do it:

1. Drink Clean – Drink plenty of clean water, at least eight to ten glasses of filtered water a day.
2. Eliminate Properly – Keep your bowels moving, at least once or twice a day. And if you can't get going, then you need some help. This can include taking two tablespoons of ground flax seeds and taking acidophilus and extra magnesium citrate capsules. If you have any chronic diseases or problems, you have to be careful about taking supplements and should work with your doctor.
3. Eat Clean – You should also eat organic produce and animal products to eliminate the toxins, hormones, and antibiotics in your food.
4. Eat Detoxifying Food – You should eat 8 to 10 servings of colorful fruits and vegetables a day, particularly family of the cruciferous vegetables (broccoli, collards, kale, cabbage, Brussels sprouts, kohlrabi) and the garlic family (garlic and onions), which help increase sulfur in the body and help detoxification.
5. Minimize Drugs – Avoid stimulants, sedatives, and drugs, such as caffeine and nicotine, and try to reduce alcohol intake.
6. Get Moving – Exercise five days a week with focus on conditioning your cardiovascular system, strengthening exercises, and stretching exercises.
7. Avoid the White Menace – This includes white flour and white sugar.
8. Sweat – Sweat profusely at least three times a week, using a sauna, steam, or a detox bath.
9. Supplement – Take a high-quality multivitamin and mineral supplement.
10. Relax – Relax deeply every day to get your nervous system in a state of calm, rest, and relaxation.

Source: Dr. Mark Hyman, MARK HYMAN, MD is dedicated to identifying and addressing the root causes of chronic illness through a groundbreaking whole-systems medicine approach called Functional Medicine. He is a family physician, a eight-time New York Times

WELCOME TO NATURE....JUMP IN TO 2014 SPRING SEASON..

This is the time for appreciation and recognition. Spring in Southern California is the magic behind everything acceptable in comparison to anywhere else. High rent, average income, spread out landscape with longer transportation time. The weather is absolute attraction between men and nature.

Although Global Warming have changed he climate everywhere, it is so much of it here as evidence especially for those who have no clue of the weather history in Southern California, as much as close to heaven on earth on a good sunny calm clear balanced day. Funny when you hear it from someone who is either a visitor from out of State, or a tourist from out of the Country, how appreciative they are to a beautiful spring day, when most of us take it for granted, and the respond that " you don't know what is it like" before, not so close but it was heaven on earth.

-MY SOCIAL CONNECTIONS

FWD.us   Moving the Knowlege Economy forward.

IMMIGRATION REFORM

Our innovative approach.

FWD.us harnesses the best of new and traditional organizing tactics. We are developing innovative technology and organizing the tech community to build an effective grassroots movement.

1. Organizing - combining both online and offline organizing tactics. Volunteer
2. Code Squad - our Code Squad program engages volunteer engineers to build the best tools in direct advocacy.
3. Partnerships - we've partnered with leading organizations across the country to organize major events.

Southern California Immigration Atorney

Riverside...www.us**law**centeronline.com/·
Southern California immigration attorneys at U.S. Law Center represent clients nationwide from offices in Riverside County and Orange County.

Why immigration reform matters.

- 11 million undocumented immigrants are left without a pathway to citizenship. That's equivalent to the population of Ohio.

- 2.1 million DREAMers were brought to the U.S. as children and are left without a way to become citizens.
- 1.4 million jobs would be created across the country if we passed immigration reform.
- $897 billion amount immigration reform would reduce the federal deficit over 20 years. $329 billion would be added to the American economy if DREAMers were given citizens.

Los Angeles Immigration Attorney- Your Immigration Solutions

Robert L. Reeves
Pasadena, California
phone (800) 795-8009
fax (626) 795-6999

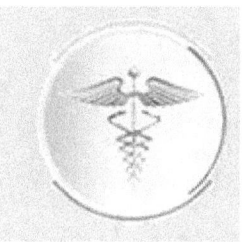

MyMedicalMalpracticeInsurance.com

MyMedicalMalpracticeInsurance
Free Quotes.
Complimentary Practice Tools.
First-Class Service.

We represent the leading 'A' rated insurers in all 50 states and we can provide you with no cost, no obligation quotations for med mal insurance specifically tailored to your needs. With our extensive

resources, you can be assured that we're prepared to show you the most cost-effective solution to your medical malpractice coverage requirements. Regardless of your location or field of specialty, we will always show you the best price and coverage to be found.

Medifast Weight Control Centers:Good for you in so man way

The program:

Simple and effective

Medifast's Products and Programs are designed to help you lose weight quickly and safely, with clinically proven meal replacements and simple plans designed with busy lifestyles in mind.

www.**medifast**centers.com/·
Welcome to Medifast Weight Control Centers Official Site.
Medifast's products and programs are designed to help you lose weight quickly and

safely.

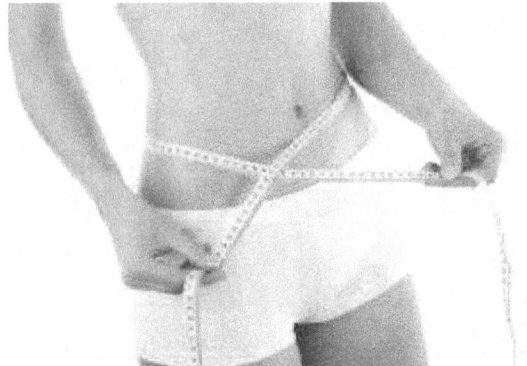 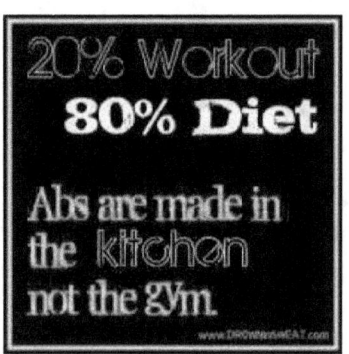

Greatest Values and Savings on Appliances

*

SHOP BY CATEGORY
*   Refrigerators
*   Washers & Dryers
*   Cooking Appliances
*   Dishwashers
*   Freezers
*   Mini Refrigerators
*   Beverage, Keg & Wine Coolers
*   Air Conditioners
*   Dehumidifiers
*   Small Appliances
*   Vacuums & Floorcare
*   Appliance Parts & Filters
*   Garbage Disposals

AA- America Anywhere Buy/Sell and other services. Free Classifieds.   NEWS U.S. JOURNAL, nusjournal.com online free classifieds.

 you find it in the computers category:

> for sale > computers

Results for computers 1 - 30 of 203

Sort by New listed Lowest price first Highest price first

	TOSHIBA TECRA A11-1HP	$ 150
	HERE IM SELLING MY USED BUT VERY GOOD CONDITION TOSHIBA TECRA A11-1HP, INTEL CORE I3 2.53GHZ, 500GB HDD, 4GB RAM, WINDOWS 7 PROFESSIONAL, MINT CONDITION COMES WITH ORIGINAL CHARGER	
	computers1 day ago	

	HP MINI NETBOOK Hp mini very clean like new coms with charger 1gb ram Hdd 320 gb,over 3.5 hours battery,wireless,web cam integratet,hd audio,sd cart windows 7 sp1 orginal with recovery parttion.i buy a ipad air and dont need any more this netbook. computers2 days ago	$ 150
	3 computer monitors, 2 keyboard, 1 mouse 3 dell computer monitors 2x15" and 1x13", 2 keyboards, 1 mouse, all in working order, all leads connected, used condition, job lot or can separate if wished. computers5 days ago	$ 50
	Apple iMac 21.5" Intel Core i5 2.5ghz 8GB ram PRICE AS STATED, NO OFFERS NO SWAPS OR EXCHANGES CASH/BANK TRANSFER ON COLLECTION ONLY NO POSTING OR SHIPPING Mid 2011 model 512mb Graphics card 3 Months Return to Base warranty Condition: The iMac is in very good condition.... computers6 days ago	$ 550
	Acer aspire 7715z 17.3 screen Acer aspire 7715z 17.3 widescreen Windows 7 Webcam2gb of ram 160g hdd Full office 07 Charger computers1 week ago	$ 150
	Refurbish laptop working on an intel core2 duo processor Rm laptop for sale. It is a refurbish laptop that has been fully tested and works like a new computer, why waste money buying a new one ? It comes with windows 7 ultimate, intel core 2 duo processor(fast working... computers1 week ago	$ 150
	Apple MacBook Pro with Retina display - 15.4" - Core i7 - OS X 10.9 Mavericks A groundbreaking Retina display. All-flash architecture. The latest Intel processors. Remarkably thin and light design. Together, these features take the notebook to a place it's never been. And they'll do the same for everything you create with it. When you... computers2 weeks ago	$ 1600
	BRAND NEW sealed box, Sony Vaio Fit Sony Vaio Fit 13 A Intel® Core™ i5 Processor, 8Gb RAM, 128Gb Hard Drive, 13 inch Touchscreen Convertible Laptop - Black First and foremost, it's a productive and entertaining VAIO® that's packed with uncompromising features. Speed through daily documents... computers2 weeks ago	$ 0

	HP ProBook 6460b 14 inch Widescreen Laptop. Windows7 Pro. Brand HP Item Weight 2 Kg Product Dimensions 45.6 x 35.8 x 11 cm Form Factor Portable Screen Size 14 inches Processor Brand Intel Processor Type Intel Core i5 Processor Speed 2.3 GHz Processor Count 2 RAM Size 6 GB... computers2 weeks ago	$ 250
	Macbook pro Retina 15" For sale my beloved Macbook pro Retina 15.4" Late 2013 (Latest) witch is a Quad i7 2.6 ghz Intel, 16gb ram, 1TB SSD, NVIDIA GeForce GT 750M with 2GB GDDR5 also APPLE CARE 3 YEARS protection plan from late 2013... computers3 weeks ago	$ 0
	COMPAQ HP 1825 18-Inch LCD Colour Monitor Very good condition 18" hp monitor, with the following specs: Brand HP Model 1825 Display Technology LCD Screen Size 18.1" Maximum Resolution 1280 x 1024 Aspect Ratio 5:4 Contrast Ratio 350:1 Response Time 30 ms Refresh Rate 75 Hz... computers3 weeks ago	Please contact
	computer desk computer desk.handle missing on left door but still very good condition.in inches it is 36 wide,19 front to back and 30 high.all accessories on it not included left on to show what can fit.cash and collection only.may negotiate price due... computers3 weeks ago	Please contact
	Laptop Toshiba Satellite psl-10e Laptop Toshiba Satellite psl-10e Intel Celron 1.4Ghz DVD/RW 1GB Ram 60GB Hard drive 15in Screen Fresh install of genuine Windows XP Installed some nice software including Microsoft Office Pro suite Ashampoo Burning Studio Pro Uniblue Speed Up my... computers3 weeks ago	$ 70
	Apple Macbook Pro 13", 2010, in excellent condition. 2010 Macbook, has had very light usage. Primarily it has been a backup computer and hence shows little sign of use. The power supply is scuffed though as it sat on the floor underneath the desk. Complete with original discs... computers3 weeks ago	$ 500

	Dell Latitude D600 The Dell Latitude D600 is a solid business system with good features and machinery. Electro computer Warehouse brings another astonishing deal of Dell Latitude D600. We are providing you the best deal at cheap rates. Intel Mobile Centrino - 1.4GHz Processor, 1GB... computers4 weeks ago	$ 150
	Compaq Tower Fully Refurbished Compaq Tower Windows Vista Home Premium Intel Pentium Dual CPU E2140 1.60ghz 2gb ram 160gb hard drive cdrw / dvdrw usb 2.0 firewire sd card reader windows media centre mouse and keyboard included - 6 months rtb warranty. ... computers4 weeks ago	$ 100
	Dell PowerEdge700 computer, Pentium 4 2.8 GHz Dell PowerEdge700 computer, Pentium 4 2.8 GHz, 2GB, 120GB Sata, CD-R/W DVD-ROM, 17in Flat Panel monitor, Windows XP Pro, Office 2007 Pro, Nero etc Keyboard & Mouse. Detail: Dell PowerEdge700 desktop computer with good quality 17 inch TFT LCD... computers4 weeks ago	$ 80
	Beautiful Acer TouchScreen Laptop This is a fantastic little laptop which is fast,slim and Light and it is also a TouchScreen Laptop and is very quiet. I am selling this Laptop as i am trying to put together some money to get a... computers5 weeks ago	$ 700
	Macbook pro Retina 15" Late 2013, Quad i7 2.7 ghz, 16gb ram For sale my beloved Macbook pro Retina 15.4" Late 2013 witch is a Quad i7 2.7 ghz, 16gb ram, 512 SSD, NVIDIA GeForce GT 750M with 2GB GDDR5 also APPLE CARE 3 YEARS protection plan from late 2013 starting till... computers6 weeks ago	$ 0
	HP NX6325 WiFi Enabled 15" Screen AMD Sempron 1GB RAM FULLY WORKING, HP Compaq AMD Sempron 3500 laptop in excellent condition. Internet ready via the onboard Ethernet Port (wired) or the onboard Mini PCI Wireless Card (WiFi). The battery holds 2hr 30min charge. Does NOT have... computers6 weeks ago	$ 120

	iMac 20" , 2.4 GHz CPU , 4GB Ram and 1 TB HDD Selling my beloved 20" iMac. Bought new and I've upgraded all possible specs from the original (built to order). The model no is "MA877LL" with RAM upgraded to 4GB and HDD to 1 TB. CPU: 2.4GHz Intel Core... computers7 weeks ago	$ 400
	Acer V5-571 Laptop Ultra Slim Core i3 Window 8 Acer v5-571 Ultra-book in excellent condition. Hard drive 500 GB Ram 4 GB Core i3 window 8 15.6" screen CD/DVD Rewriter. 15.6" Screen. I got 2 of them laptop. blue colour usb port.manual book. Comes with charger. computers7 weeks ago	$ 300
	Imac 21.5 inch 2012 Brand new only taken out of box once, factory settings comes with all original boxing mouse keyboard etc computers7 weeks ago	$ 800
	Fujitsu Seimens laptopWindows 7 All working has charger and bag 1gb windows 7 wifi dvd r. computers8 weeks ago	$ 78
	Custom PC Intel QuadCore 10Ghz, Wifi Keyboard The PC has a very fastionable case/tower with custom upgraded hardware and software This is custom made and is very fast and clean and cannot be bought in the shop This PC has built in Wifi so you can... computers8 weeks ago	$ 500
	Apple iMac 21.5 - Intel 3.06Ghz Up for sale is my Apple iMac 21.5inch Intel 3.06Ghz and Pre-loaded with Multimedia Software. (No Keyboard or Mouse) - Just the unit for sale. The imac is in good condition, does have a couple of cosmetic marks here... computers8 weeks ago	$ 500
	Mini-ITX Gaming PC - Liquid Cooled Intel Core i5 3570K 4.0GHz, 8GB Memory, GTX 770, 1TB SSHD This is a Mini-ITX Gaming PC - Perfect for hooking up to your Monitor as a general use Gaming PC or even your TV, as a fantastic Home Theatre Gaming PC. I've made a very modest overclock on the... computers8 weeks ago	$ 700

	24" Acer LED Monitor S240HL Full HD, VGA/DVI/HDMI, Great Condition Selling 24" monitor in great condition, with very minor scuffs that go unnoticed and a very small scratch (around 1 cm) on the screen that cannot be seen when the monitor is on, and difficult to see, if not find,... computers8 weeks ago	$ 30
	Dell inspiron 1564 intel core i3/4gb ram/250gb hdd selling my dell Inspiron 1564 laptop fully working comes with original dell charger and a laptop carrying bag only selling due to getting a macbook specs: check pics for more details intel core i3 2.13ghz, 2.13ghz 4 Gb... computers9 weeks ago	$ 250
	APPLE MACBOOK PRO 13INCHES APPLE MACBOOK PRO 13INCHES 2.5GHZ -4GBRAM-250GB-MAVERICKS OPERATING SYSTEM OFFICE 2011-ILIFE 2011 - LOGIC PRO - TURN UP -VIRTUALDJ COME APPLE CHARGER FINAL CUT PRO- TOAST 11- SOUND TRACK PRO - ADBOE CS6 AS FOLLOWS ADBOE ENCORE -... computers9 weeks ago	$ 500

Feature Story "*La Opinión*"

EVERY CHILD DESERVES A QUALITY PUBLIC SCHOOL EDUCATION.

Only 56% of our students at Los Angeles Unified School District graduate high school on time

"DON'T HOLD US BACK"

La Opinión is a Spanish-language daily newspaper published in Los Angeles, California, USA and distributed throughout the six counties of Southern California. It is the largest Spanish-language newspaper in the United States and second-most read newspaper in Los Angeles (after *The Los Angeles Times*). It is published by Impremedia LLC. Its Impremedia shares are held by Lozano Enterprises, the private equity company of the Lozano family. The newspaper is headquartered in Suites 3000 and 3100 in the MCI Center in Downtown Los Angeles.

The Lozanos continued to be involved in the operations of the newspaper. Leticia Lozano, the eldest child of Ignacio E. Lozano, Jr., worked at *La Opinión* from 1976 to 1984, at which point she got married and moved to Italy. Her younger brother, José Ignacio Lozano, was named Assistant Publisher in 1977 and Publisher in 1986. In 2004, *La Opinión* merged with New York City-based *El Diario La Prensa*, the oldest Spanish-language newspaper in the United States, to form ImpreMedia LLC. José Lozano became Vice chairman of the new parent company, and his sister, Monica C. Lozano, also serves as Senior Vice President of Impremedia LLC. In 2004, Mónica Lozano, was named Publisher and CEO of *La Opinión*. Monica Lozano's younger brother, Francisco Lozano, was promoted to Impremedia's corporate director of magazines in 2007. He previously worked as Sales Development Director for Impremedia and as National Sales Manager for *La Opinión*.

All Lozano family assets, Lozano Enterprises, are wrapped up in Impremedia, which was formed from the combination of Lozano Enterprises and CPK Media, in 2004. Impremedia LLC is the first national Spanish-language newspaper company.

In May 2012, the Lozano family sold controlling interest in La Opinion to the Argentine newspaper La Nacion. Monica Lozano and the staff of La Opinion remain, but the family no longer controls the newspaper.

The paper was first founded and published on September 16, 1926 by Ignacio E. Lozano, Sr.. He emigrated from Mexico to San Antonio, Texas in 1908 where Lozano first founded a Spanish language daily newspaper known as *La Prensa* in 1913.

With the increase in the Mexican population Los Angeles experienced during the 1920s, Lozano believed he had a strong base for a Spanish newspaper in the growing city and founded *La Opinión* on September 16 to coincide with Mexico's Independence Day. The Lozano family retained control over both *La Prensa* and *La Opinion* until 1959 when *La Prensa* was sold.

In its early existence *La Opinión* consisted primarily of news from Mexico to accommodate the reading preferences of its audience, made up in large part by recently emigrated Mexicans. *La Opinión* was one of the few newspapers to provide comprehensive coverage of the deportations and repatriations of Mexicans during the 1930s as well as the Zoot Suit Riots of the 1940s.

In 1990, 50% ownership of the paper was sold to the Times Mirror Company, which merged with the Tribune Company in 2000. In 2004, Impremedia bought Tribune Company out and regained full control over *La Opinión*.

Fairfield Inn & Suites by Marriott: Let's Get it Done

MARRIOTT.....................MARRIOTT.COM/FAIRFIELDINN AND SUITES. BOOK ONLINE..

Welcome to what you need:

Fairfield Inn & Suites

La Opinión has vastly diversified its coverage from purely Mexican to include the Central American, South American, Cuban, and Puerto Rican populations that have grown in Los Angeles over the last quarter century. It now includes reporting on issues relevant to a wide variety of Hispanics. In the words of former Publisher Ignacio E. Lozano, Jr.: *Our mission was no longer to be a Mexican newspaper published in Los Angeles, but an American newspaper that happens to be published in Spanish.*

Since 1986, *La Opinión's* editorial staff has doubled in size and the paper has grown to include bureaus in Sacramento, California, Washington DC and Mexico City. In 1999 and 2000, *La Opinión* was recognized by the National Association of Hispanic Journalists as the *Outstanding Spanish Language Daily Newspaper of the Year.*

In 2006, *La Opinión* received the highest-ranking recognition in Spanish-language journalism, the Jose' Ortega y Gasset Award from Spain's distinguished *El País* newspaper. *El País* honored *La Opinión* for its pioneering trajectory over eighty years creating and maintaining an unprecedented media outlet for the growing Hispanic population in the United States.

In November 2007, *La Opinión* ranked #1 in net daily paid circulation growth among the 200 largest newspapers in America for the six-month period ending September 2007, based on the latest FAS-FAX Report from the Audit Bureau of Circulation. The daily average is based on Monday-Friday.

However, since 2008, the staff of La Opinion has dwindled and the Impre Media empire grew weaker. As of May 2012, a subsidiary of the Argentine newspaper La Nacion purchased a majority share of

Impremedia and La Opinion.

MY PLACES CONNECTIONS

Amazing places:

O.C. day trip: Santa Ana Artists Village

Peek inside local artist studios as you stroll through Orange County's changing fall leaves......................

The Artists Village's 40-plus galleries open their doors for the First Saturday Art Walk.

Beverly Hills for the rest of us

It's not just a playground for stars. Here's how to live large on the cheap in 90210

more

Top spots for fun in East Hollywood

Tinseltown is ready for its close-up, and the star is in the east. Check out these top spots for eats, drinks, and more fun

more

Day trip: Malibu, CA

Malibu in fall: Southern California's beautiful summer weather without the summer crowds

more

One perfect day in Glendale, CA

Check out this historic L.A. suburb offering the perfect day-to-night activities

Travel»California»Best Southern California getaways

Best Southern California getaways

From the West's best theme parks to perfect, sun-drenched beach towns, you can't go wrong with these SoCal escapes

New at Disneyland in 2014

Walt Disney shows plans for Disneyland. He is quoted as saying: "Disneyland will never be completed. It will continue to grow as long as there is imagination left in the world."

Courtesy of Disneyland

9 Disneyland tips for your best-ever visit

Get advice on what to see, where to explore, and how to beat the crowds

more

Plus fun places to visit nearby:

- One perfect day in Irvine's Great Park

- One perfect day in Costa Mesa, CA

- One perfect day in San Clemente, CA

- O.C. day trip: Santa Ana Artists Village

- Day trip: Upper Newport Bay

Perfect Palm Springs summer escape

Palm Springs insummer? Yep, we said it. Zero crowds, killer deals, and a pool around every corner make this the place to be

more

Desert Hot Springs escape

Snowbirds flock to Palm Springs, but for some lower-key you time, get down to essentials in Desert Hot Springs

more

Off the beaten path in Santa Barbara

A savvy traveler shows us there's more here than State Street and the wharf·

more

One perfect day in Goleta, CA

Take a peek inside one of Southern California's most garden-friendly beach towns.

more

A day at the races in Del Mar

Pick a pony and try your luck at this SoCal stable staple

more

Day trip: Big Bear Lake

Thrill-seekers and beach bums find common ground at this Southern California hot spot

more

Temecula Valley Wine Country

Temecula, CA

www.temeculawines.org

For those of you who are of age, Temecula's a great area to go wine touring, especially if you don't have the time to make it up to **Napa**.

Reserve a hot air balloon ride for you and your better half. If that doesn't win them over, we don't

know what will!
BONUS SPOT

Old Town Pasadena

If you haven't strolled along this area of Pasadena, you're missing out. It's 22 blocks of pure delight with cafes, art galleries, and so many other wonderful things to check out.

Huntington Botanical Gardens

1151 Oxford Road

San Marino, CA 91108

Sure, you could always buy your lady a bouquet of roses, but why not just take her to an entire garden?

The botanical gardens at the **Huntington Library** are home to more than 14,000 varieties of plants and it's a great place to get in touch with nature while also catching some rays. ⊡

Santa Monica Pier

200 Santa Monica Pier

Santa Monica, CA 90401

Act like a kid again and take a trip on over to the **Santa Monica** pier. It's your one-stop shop for carnival fun.

Play some games, win a stuffed animal, and ride the Ferris wheel with your **Valentine**! ⊡

Catalina Island

Avalon, CA 90704

www.catalinachamber.com

If a day trip is more your style, **Catalina Island** may do the trick.

You can take guided tours through the wilderness, check out the historic casino, or get gorgeous view of it all by para-sail.

Ferries depart from **Long Beach**, **San Pedro**, **Dana Point**, **Newport Beach**, and **Marina del Rey** and it takes less than an hour to get there.

Southern Comfort California Little Towns

Little Saigon is a name given to any of several overseas Vietnamese immigrant and descendant communities in the United States. Saigon is the former name of the capital of the former South Vietnam, where a large number of first-generation Vietnamese immigrants originate.[1]

The most well-established and largest Vietnamese-American enclaves, not all of which are called Little

Saigon, are located in Orange County, California; San Jose, California; and Houston, Texas. Somewhat smaller communities also exist, including the comparatively nascent Vietnamese commercial districts in San Francisco, San Diego, Atlanta, Sacramento, Denver, Oklahoma City, New Orleans, the Dallas-Fort Worth Metroplex (Haltom City, Arlington, and Garland), Falls Church, Virginia and Orlando. Additionally, Vietnamese-Americans of Chinese lineage have also established businesses and bringing distinctively Vietnamese elements to most Chinatowns, essentially blurring the line between a "Chinatown" and a "Little Saigon"; some examples would include the Chinatowns of Las Vegas, Chicago, New York City, Philadelphia, Boston, Bellaire in Houston, Honolulu or Edmonton, Alberta.

Koreatown is a neighborhood in Central Los Angeles, California, centered near Eighth Street and Western Avenue[2] but with disputed borders.

According to the *Los Angeles Times,* it is the most densely populated district by population in Los Angeles County, with some 120,000 residents in 2.7 square miles. It is highly diverse ethnically, with half of the residents being Latino and a third being Asian. Two-thirds of the residents were born outside of the United States, a high figure compared to the rest of the city.

The neighborhood culture has historically been highly specific to the Korean-background population, although more recently there has been an increasing interaction between Koreans and Latinos in Koreatown as the Latino population is now booming.[3] There is a Korean Festival and Parade as well as a city park called Seoul International and a Koreatown shopping center, a Korean Education Center and the Koreatown Workers Alliance.

Koreatown is home to the Robert F. Kennedy Community Schools, built on the property of the former Ambassador Hotel, where Senator Robert F. Kennedy was assassinated in 1968, and thirteen other primary or secondary schools, as well as a law school.

A special graphics district has been established within the Koreatown borders. There are three Metro subway stops in the area.

Little Armenia is a community that is part of the Hollywood district of Los Angeles, California. It falls within the area referred to as East Hollywood. The area is served by the Metro Red Line at the Hollywood/Western station.

Little Armenia is defined by the Los Angeles City Council as "the area bounded on the north by Hollywood Boulevard between the 101 Freeway and Vermont Avenue, on the east by Vermont Avenue from Hollywood Boulevard to Santa Monica Boulevard, on the south by Santa Monica Boulevard between Vermont Avenue and U.S. Route 101 and on the west by Route 101 from Santa Monica Boulevard to Hollywood Boulevard" (adopted on 6 October 2000).[1] It also overlaps substantially with Thai Town.

We Connect 2 Business Directory at weconnect2.com and digital network.

advertisers to reach additional audiences on our award-winning search marketing platform.
Arts and crafts

Hampshire

Traders
An online store selling oil paintings and other works of art.
http://www.hampshiretraders.com

Automobile
Interstateautoclub
club members have it all, towing, insurance, auto show, and advertising.
http:www.interstateautoclub.co

Business

weconnect2media
public relation, group of companies producing, publishing, and education outreach.
http//:www.weconnect2.com

Arizona Business Professionals
Search a directory of Arizona business professionals including Lawyers, Accountants, Architects, Realtors, and more.
http://www.azbizpros.com

Blue Boomerang - Business Directory
Search the Blueboomerang directory guide for a wide range of business listings covering a variety of areas.
http://www.blueboomerang.comt

Business Directory
Local Search 24 is a business directory for the Norfolk region. The directory lists many businesses from many different industries.
http://www.localsearch24.co.uk

eMetro411 Houston Texas
An information portal and business directory for residents and small business owners in Houston Texas.
http://www.emetro411.com

Fuzing.com
An international business to business (b2b) trade portal that helps buyers and suppliers of goods and services to overcome the major hurdle of locating suitable trading partners.
http://www.fuzing.com

Houston Business Directory
A web directory for Houston businesses who need to advertise their website on the internet and web.

http://www.houston-area.com

Investing In China
Submit and read new investment and business opportunities in China, consult a directory of Chinese manufacturers and investment companies.
http://www.investinginchina.co.uk

Careers

policewithoutborders
police community news and feud, public relation, and multimedia advertising.
http//:www.policewithoutborders.com
Computer

Education
National Universe Students Journal
college and universities studens participation in the community.
http//:www.nusjournal
Entertainment

World Mentoring Academy
FREE Interactive Learning OpenCourseware
from MIT, UC Berkeley, Harvard, Yale, Stanford, U Houston, USC, UCLA, Khan ...
http//:www.worldmentoringacademy.com

Health and Fitness

Fitness First Gyms, Download Free Pass
Get a free Fitness First gym pass and check out gym membership offers at the local gym.
http://www.fitnessfirst.co.uk/

Garmin Edge 500

Athleti offers a range of endurance sports equipment including some of the latest Garmin products.
http://www.athleti.ca

Health and Fitness

Tennis, gyms, swimming, wet spas and more at the UK based David Lloyd Leisure Group health and fitness club.
http://www.davidlloyd.co.uk/

Klick Fitness
fitness club, Klick Fitness have several gyms throughout the UK with cardiovascular and strength training machines available.
http://www.klickfitness.com

Personal Trainer Richmond Hill
Toronto Fitness Online offers personal training sessions around the Greater Toronto area.
http://www.torontofitnessonline.com/

Health and fitness sports magazine
online magazine featuring articles, advertising, events, and resources for sports and recreation, fitness and exercise, health and wellness.
www.healthfitnessmag.com

Home and Garden
visions in furniture
experience, personable, value
all your furniture needs.
http//:www.visionsinfurnitureinc.com

Law Offices

You can trust the experience of our office when deciding to file for bankruptcy. Whether it is a Chapter 7 bankruptcy to eliminate credit card debt, or a Chapter 13 bankruptcy to help save your home from foreclosure and eliminate a second mortgage - See more at::
http://aibrahimlaw.com/

Lifestyle and Romance

Money and Finance

Publishing

Anaheim Publishing

custom publishing and media, books online, articles and short stories, press releases, advertising online, special design of marketing and advertising campaign materials on line.
http//:www.anaheimpublishing.co
Reference

Custom publishing

custom media, & Custom magazines for high impact branding & relationship marketing. Exclusive distribution channels for B2B marketing.
http//:www.custompublishingne.com

Society

Sports

Sport Business Digestt
sport news online. uptodate ranking of sport figures.
hhtp//::wwww.sportsbusinessdigest.com

Toys Games

Travel
http//:wwww.hotwire.com/
Tripadvisor_Reviews of hotels, flights and vacation Rentals
unbiased hotel reviews, photos and travel advice for hotels and vacations.

www.hotwire.com/

Please submit directory form, indicate desired category next to your business name A for Arts and Crafts E for Education, see example under Arts and Crafts, check back within 7 days.

FUNNY PHOTOS

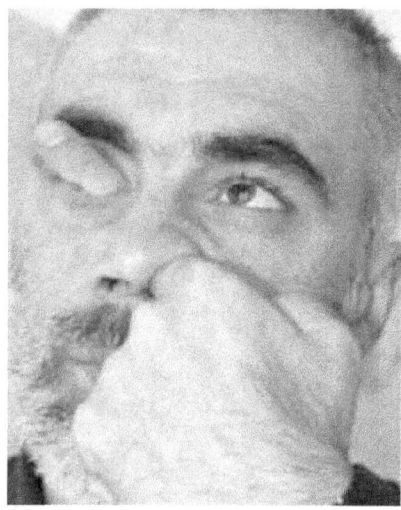

My Fashion Connections:

Spring Fashion That Makes a Statement

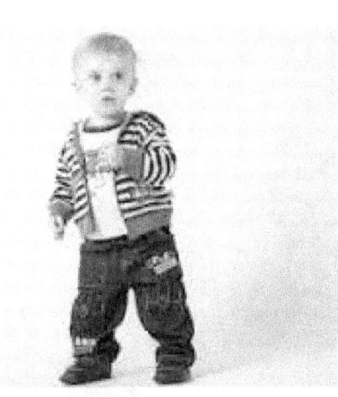

FASHION

IS A STATEMENT, NOT A STYLE. FASHION DOES NOT HAVE TO BE WORN CASUALLY, NOR OUTSIDE THE RUNWAY. FASHION IS FIT FOR ALL SIZES FOR ALL PEOPLE OF ALL AGES. FASHION IS AN ART OF PERSONAL SELF-EXPRESSION, NOT AN EXCUSE TO BE PRETTY, POPULAR AND CHARISMATIC.

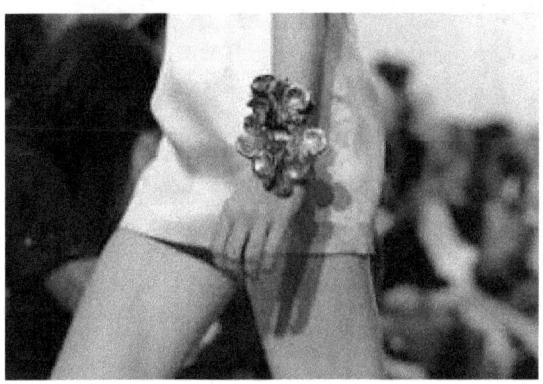

THIS SPRING FASHION STATEMENT

SPRING

Fashion Preview

2014

AA- America Anywhere Buy/Sell and other services. Free Classified.

From News U.S. Journal online nusjournal.com. For Sale Sports, Bikes :

Sort by New listed Lowest price first Highest price first

![]	**Custom Merida Big nine Carbon XT Edition** 2013 Big Nine Carbon dual suspension XC bike size Medium 17 inch Less than 12 months old serviced by BNG in Townsville Selling due to change in style of bikes looking to go a carbon hardtail for 2014 Upgrades Include... sports, bikes14 weeks ago	$ 2500
![]	**Bench Press** Condition: newIn new condition as picture,no weights included,firm price only sports, bikes14 weeks ago	$ 150
![]	**power ranges cat class 16 inch** This is a Power Ranger cat clash 16 inch tires training wheels great shape any questions email me. sports, bikes16 weeks ago	$ 15
![]	**Trek 930 Single-Track mountain bike** Trek 930 for sale, full specs here: http://bikepedia.com/QuickBike/BikeSpecs.aspx?Year=1994&Brand=Trek&Model=930&Type=bike#.Ur4Ywn-9KSM Cost over 550 in 1994, clean, solid black frame, these USA made bikes will last forever. 18in frame fits 5'7-6ft. Upgraded Bontrager 26in slick/city tires sports, bikes16 weeks ago	$ 150

	**Small frame ladies bike with child seat** Used this as a station bike. Can use a tune up but can ride as it. Baby seat is an older model and small, would not fit anyone bigger than 2 years sports, bikes28 weeks ago	$ 25
	21 Speed Diamondback Peak It's a small frame so you would have to be shorter than 5'6" to ride this bike. Has front and under the seat shocks and smooth street tires. Good condition. sports, bikes29 weeks ago	$ 60
	Fuji Classic Track Bike Fuji Classic 61cm Track Bike. Used, but in great shape. Includes the original drop handlebars with secondary brake leavers added. Also, new Odyssey pedals. sports, bikes29 weeks ago	$ 400
	Fuji Palisade 12 speed 65 CM Please leave a number if you email me. Mint condition, tuned, greased and ready to ride with a 25" frames. sports, bikes30 weeks ago	$ 280

La Opinión" inside. Feature Story Spring 14

FASHION
IS A STATEMENT, NOT A STYLE. FASHION DOES NOT HAVE TO BE WORN CASUALLY, NOR OUTSIDE THE RUNWAY. FASHION IS FIT FOR ALL SIZES FOR ALL PEOPLE OF ALL AGES. FASHION IS AN ART OF PERSONAL SELF-EXPRESSION, NOT AN EXCUSE TO BE PRETTY, POPULAR AND CHARISMATIC.

News U.S. Journal nusjournal.com free classified For Sale, Jobs, Cars, Apartment, and more.

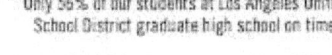

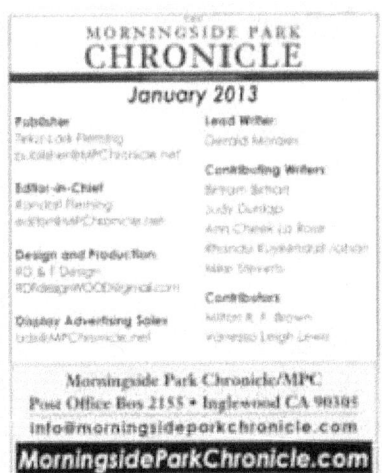

From We Connect 2 Publishing and Digital Network another in print publication for sale at amazon.com and hp magcloud.com look for special offer with free shipping from amazon.

Why not a digital copy of Connections Magazine for a lot less, and make it a gift to a friend and family.

We are online all the time myconnectionsmagazine.com We are as far yuppy you can get.

Free Coupons

Disneyland Ticket Coupons and Deals from ShopAtHome.com!

	Get Disne yland Ticket Coup ons and more!

"I never order anything online without going to ShopAtHome.com first. They have great coupons, coupon codes and promotions for almost any store you can think of. In addition to that, you earn rebates on most of the orders you place. What a great way to shop; not only do you save money on your order you also receive a rebate check in the mail. It's almost like getting paid to shop!"

Rachel, Columbus, OH

-MY PLACES CONNECTIONS

MAY 31 IS SET FOR THE GRAND OPENING OF THE ANAHEIM PACKING HOUSE.

Anaheim Brewery's Anniversary and Friedrich Conrad's Birthday Smash-Up

Anaheim Brewery's first 50 years ran from 1870 up to 1920, when National Prohibition closed the taps. I'm proud to say that while other cities voted themselves dry years before the Volstead Act, Anaheim stayed *wet* until the last possible day.

After a 90-year hangover, we finally got around to re-opening the brewery and beer garden about a mile away from the old one. We've been in our new spot for 3 years now.

If 53 total years in business wasn't reason enough to party, it's also Fred Conrad's birthday.

Friedrich Conrad ran Anaheim Brewery from the mid-1870s till 1904. He was born in Bavaria in 1849 and came to California as a teenager We like him so much we put his picture on our Anaheim Hefeweizen

and every spring we brew him up a special batch of "Conrad's Kölsch."

Let's raise a glass to 53 more years of Famous Anaheim Beer and party like we're 165!

The Anaheim Packing District proudly announces the Grand Opening of the highly anticipated, newly restored Anaheim Packing House, a community gathering place and OC's first food hall celebrating its rich agricultural history. More than 20 hand-selected culinary artisans will open their doors including a fresh veggie stand, juicery, butcher, baker, handcrafted sandwich shop, fresh seafood, Indian fare, pizzeria, coffee shop and chocolatier, among others, all of which will serve in a communal dining hall that spills to outside covered porches on rail cars. To celebrate the culmination of a decade of restoration and the repurposing of this 1919 citrus packing house, the Anaheim Packing District is hosting a Grand Opening festival free to the public and spanning the Anaheim Packing House, Farmers

Park, and the restored Packard dealership at 440 S. Anaheim Blvd., Anaheim, on May 31 from 12 p.m. to 10 p.m.

The official ribbon cutting ceremony will take place at 1 p.m. on the front steps with Anaheim Mayor, Tom Tait, officiating. Local stakeholders and history buffs will act as honorary docents for the day and provide tours of the historical landmark.

The all-day celebration will feature live music from various country and blue grass bands, line dancing lessons, hosted kids games and crafts on the Park, afternoon hay rides, free lemonade, popcorn and lite bites, as well as commemorative giveaways while supplies last.

According to a **Little Arabia (Anaheim, California)** Facebook page,] local Arab Americans are seeking to promote and improve local businesses, partner with the City of Anaheim to revitalize Brookhurst Street, and promote this area to those outside Anaheim as a cultural destination.

The district is centered on Brookhurst Street in Anaheim, near the Santa Ana Freeway (I-5) between La Palma Avenue and Katella Avenue. Businesses includehalal butcher shops, beauty salons, jewelry stores, travel agencies, bakeries,] Arab, Armenian, and restaurants, and hookah cafes. There are also numerous mosques and a few churches in the enclave.

Little Arabia is known for its popular hookah lounges. More than a dozen businesses that serve hookah and/or sells hookah supplies exist in the district. Popular hookah lounges include Hidden Cafe, Fusion Ultra Lounge, Dream Cafe. Restaurants that serve hookah include Nubia Cafe, Al-Waha

BBQ, Andaluz, Nara Bistro, Pita Paradise, and others. Anaheim made national news in 2005 when the city banned belly dancing in Little Arabia's hookah bars

An Unusual Fat Loss Story

After years of struggle, we stumbled on what many now believe is the simplest, quickest and safest way to burning the fat. We'll show you the solution, and how something that happened with our kids changed everything...WATCH THE FREE PRESENTATION ONLINE AT

zerotoherofitness.com

1 Fat That Fights Belly Fat

Knowing which fats make you fatter and which ones help you strip away flab is key in your weight loss success. We'll show you 1 unique fat that specfically targets stubborn flab like belly fat when you eat more of it...

2 Foods To Never Eat

There are some foods that are on millions of dinner and restaurant tables right now that you should never eat. We'll show you 2 specific "weight loss" foods that in reality make it even more difficult to burn fat and keep it off...

Our Mission

Our mission at Zero to Hero Fitness is to help you to finally lose the weight and keep it off, strengthen your body and mind, and experience naturally high levels of energy throughout the day. Our products and methods are designed to be as simple as possible, but not simpler. Our education is direct, personal and puts efficiency first and foremost. We believe everyone, regardless of your past or current struggles with your health or fitness, can greatly improve on your existing condition and live life in your best body possible.

Our company was founded with two important principles: First, as an informational resource for weight loss, diet, fitness and other health related topics. Secondly, we aim to entertain while educating our readers. We understand that it can be difficult to get yourself focused enough to learn what you need to in order to change your body, health and life for the better - so we do our very best to present our content in the most engaging ways possible.

> **3 "Healthy" Foods To Avoid**
> Did you know that many foods marketed to you as "healthy" can actually cause you to store more body fat? We'll show you 3 surprising foods you should avoid if you care about losing stubborn flab like belly fat...

Don't forget to watch the entire presentation because it's full of free fat burning tips you can use right away, and we save the best for last!

Little Arabia – Anaheim is an ethnic enclave in Orange County, California, United States, the center for Orange County's Arab-Americans, who number more than 24,000 (As of 2000). It is sometimes referred to as "Little Gaza" which was a play on the original designation of this area as the "Garza Island." Little Arabia grew significantly in the 1990s with the arrival of immigrants from the Middle East, and is the home thousands of Arab-Americans predominantly hailing from Egypt, Syria and Palestine.

Little Saigon is a name given to ethnic enclaves of expatriate Vietnamese mainly in English-speaking free countries. Alternate names include **Little Vietnam** and **Little Hanoi** (mainly in historically communist nations), depending on the enclave's political history. Saigon is the former name of the capital of the former South Vietnam, where a large number of first-generation Vietnamese immigrants arriving to the United States originate,[1] whereas Hanoi is the current capital of Vietnam.

The most well-established and largest Vietnamese-American enclaves, not all of which are called Little Saigon, are located in Orange County, California; San Jose, California; and Houston, Texas. Somewhat smaller communities also exist, including the comparatively nascent Vietnamese commercial districts in San Francisco, San Diego, Atlanta,Sacramento, Denver, Oklahoma City, New Orleans, the Dallas-Fort Worth Metroplex (Haltom City, Arlington, andGarland), Falls Church, Virginia and Orlando. Additionally, Vietnamese-Americans of Chinese lineage have also established businesses and bringing distinctively Vietnamese elements to most Chinatowns, essentially blurring the line between a "Chinatown" and a "Little Saigon"; some examples would include the Chinatowns of Las Vegas, Chicago, New York City, Philadelphia, Boston, Bellaire inHouston, Honolulu or Edmonton, Alberta.

The Top 10 Best Restaurant Places to Eat in Southern California

Pink's

The original 1939 Pink's (pinkshollywood.com) hot dog stand is in Hollywood, drawing massive lines all day and late into the evening. Unique hot dog selections include the bacon burrito dog, mushroom Swiss dog and the Lord of the Rings dog topped with barbecue sauce and onion rings.

Musso and Frank Grill

Founded in 1919, Musso & Frank Grill (mussoandfrank.com), the oldest restaurant in Hollywood, offers up such classic American fare as roasted lamb, porterhouse steak and broiled lobster. The old-fashioned decor includes red leather booths, white linens and waiters dressed in red tuxedos.

The Original Tommy's

Featuring more than 30 locations throughout Southern California, The Original Tommy's (originaltommys.com) began in 1946 as a lone Los Angeles hamburger joint. Located on the corner of Beverly and Rampart, the original shack still stands and serves burgers, hot dogs and French fries topped with the restaurant's famed chili.

Philippe the Original

Located at the edge of LA's Chinatown, Philippe the Original (philippes.com) opened its doors back in 1908. The menu includes a variety of fresh-baked pies, deli salads and the restaurant's famed French dipped beef, turkey, pork, ham and lamb sandwiches. Diners enjoy meals at communal wooden tables atop sawdust-covered floors.

The Original Pantry Cafe

Open 24 hours, The Original Pantry Cafe (pantrycafe.com) is in the heart of downtown L.A., just a few short blocks from Staples Center. Founded in 1924, the restaurant features long lines in the morning, but breakfast is served all day. Hearty offerings include eggs, pancakes, thick cuts of toast and biscuits with gravy.

Canter's Deli

Canter's Deli (cantersdeli.com) first opened in 1931. Situated in LA's Fairfax district, the Jewish deli offers such fare as pastrami sandwiches, matzo ball soup, roasted brisket and a variety of baked goods. Attached to the deli, The Kibitz Room features a cocktail lounge and small stage for musical acts. The restaurant remains open 24 hours.

In-N-Out

Perhaps the most famous burger joint in Southern California, In-N-Out (in-n-out.com) features a basic menu complete with burgers, fries and milkshakes. Locals know the lingo for off-the-menu items, including the four-by-four (hamburgers with four patties), protein-style (hamburgers with lettuce wraps instead of bread) and the Flying Dutchman (a grilled cheese with hamburger patties instead of bread).

Encounter Restaurant and Bar

Encounter Restaurant and Bar (encounterlax.com) sits atop LAX's funky space-themed structure in the airport parking lot. An elevator equipped with space-age music and colorful lights transports diners to the main hall. The kitschy, 1960s throwback restaurant features fare like grilled fish and poultry, blue lava lamps at the bar and views of departing and arriving planes.

Spago

Located in Beverly Hills, Wolfgang Puck's own Spago (wolfgangpuck.com) offers a bar, two private dining rooms and an open kitchen. The menu features gourmet fare like pan-roasted duck, grilled New York steak and veal schnitzel. The extensive wine list includes selections from France, Italy and Austria.

Clifton's Cafeteria

Based in downtown Los Angeles, Clifton's Cafeteria (cliftonscafeteria.com) dates back to 1935. The multi-story, woodsy-themed interior features a 20-foot tall waterfall, faux trees, giant rocks and even a prayer chapel. The cafeteria-style restaurant offers more than 100 items daily, including fruit, soups, veggies, pastas and grilled meats.

Bases on USA Today's data base.

This Spring Issue of Connections Magazine featuring a unique brreakfast place in Southern California:

Jennlfei Tedrizzi

Gimme that brekkie!

The Breakfast Bar's a Good Egg

This Long Beach restaurant is the city's latest morning haven, with a must-try, secret-recipe omelet casserole..Long Beach needs to update its official seal to include a plate of bacon and eggs. Sure, the town already has a world-class aquarium, its own Grand Prix and the Queen Mary. But its biggest attraction, in my opinion, is the never-ending array of breakfast joints where you can tuck into a meal first thing in the morning. You want pancakes? The Potholder Cafe boasts one with the circumference of an area rug. French toast? Starling Diner starts its by soaking a French baguette in crème Anglaise, baking it, then injecting it with mascarpone. A genuine diner experience? Jongewaard's Bake-N-Broil is a modern Rockwellian landmark serving three square meals a day and slices of pie for dessert.

And then there's the newest entrant: the Breakfast Bar, which serves a morning item unlike any Long Beach has seen before. Owners Josh and Pamela Beadel call it an omelet casserole, but it's neither an omelet nor a casserole. Since it dissipates like an eggy cloud in your mouth, it most closely resembles a cheese soufflé. Ask your waitress about it, and she reveals the recipe: a piece of bread soaked overnight with egg, cheese and milk, then baked in an au gratin dish.

"Most people don't even taste the bread," she adds. And she's right. But learning the secret ingredient somehow makes the omelet casserole that much more mysteriously magical. It also makes you grateful the Beadels, who used to work for George's Greek Cafe and Congregation Ale House, decided to set out on their own and transform a shuttered Mexican joint attached to a motel into this place, if only to ensure there was an outlet for this dish. The recipe, the menu says, has been passed down for three generations, invented by a great-uncle named Marcee. He gets full credit on the menu, but the potato pancake it's served with is entirely attributable to a kitchen that knows a breakfast potato side dish has to be simultaneously crispy, fluffy and toe-curlingly steamy. The potato patty is all these things, making it the casserole's equal, with the outer-crust crunchiness of a tater tot and the interior temperature of a baked potato, requiring nothing else except maybe a dash of hot sauce.

If there's another potato-based dish that could compete with it, it's the Hung Over, which is listed in the appetizer section because the Everest of hot fries smothered in cheese-laced scrambled eggs, cut-up sausage, gravy, onions, peppers, pico de gallo and spiced sour cream is designed to be shared. Yet, if you're there by yourself, sitting in one of the semi-secluded back booths, you might realize the scrambled eggs are also miraculous—creamy, wiggly, with just the right amount of wet—and it'd be a shame if you didn't finish it all right there, your plans for lunch and dinner be damned.

It's also about then, as you sip the invigorating cucumber lemonade—a specialty cocktail made with soju and enough cucumber curls to qualify as a salad—that you survey the scene. The Breakfast Bar has been open for less than six months, yet it already has a cast of regulars, their heads buried behind newspapers. On weekend mornings, there are likely to be hipsters, Goths, blue-haired retirees, even a few conventioneers, all devouring poached eggs smothered with Hollandaise and spinach on the sun-bathed patio. This, you realize, is why breakfast is Long Beach's most popular meal. No matter where you were last night or end up later, pancakes, eggs and bacon taste good now. Plus, these pancakes, made from freshly ground whole wheat and berries, couldn't be fluffier if they were made out of cotton balls.

Though burgers and sandwiches are offered, you see hardly anyone ordering them. Even past noon, the closest thing to lunch food the Breakfast Bar's customers consume is the breakfast guacamole or the fried chicken wings and waffles. The former has black beans in it, along with hard-boiled eggs, ground country sausage, pico de gallo, cheese and half an avocado sliced and laid down atop the molcajete—what you'd get if you merged an egg salad and a ceviche, then served it with tortilla chips. The chicken-and-waffle dish is an obvious nod to Roscoe's (blocks away), but here, the waffles are floppy, flat things you're supposed to dip into one of the three sauces. One of them, a buttered syrup, tastes like molten butterscotch. The gravy, which has strings of cheese in it, is a meal unto itself, another recipe the Beadels inherited from a family member.

Yes, Long Beach was already rich with morning food before the Breakfast Bar came into town, but it's now even more so. So let's talk about that seal.

OCWEEKLY REPORT.

Little of a lot. Little Italy:

Little Italy is a somewhat hilly neighborhood in Downtown San Diego, California that was originally a predominatelyItalian fishing neighborhood. It has since been gentrified and now Little Italy is a scenic neighborhood composed mostly of Italian restaurants, Italian retail shops, home design stores, art galleries, and residential units.

Little Italy is one of the more active downtown neighborhoods and has frequent festivals and events including a weekly farmers market, also known as the *Mercato* (the Market, in Italian). The neighborhood has low crime rates when compared with other neighborhoods in Downtown San Diego and is maintained by the Little Italy Neighborhood Association, which looks after trash

collection, decorations, and special events.

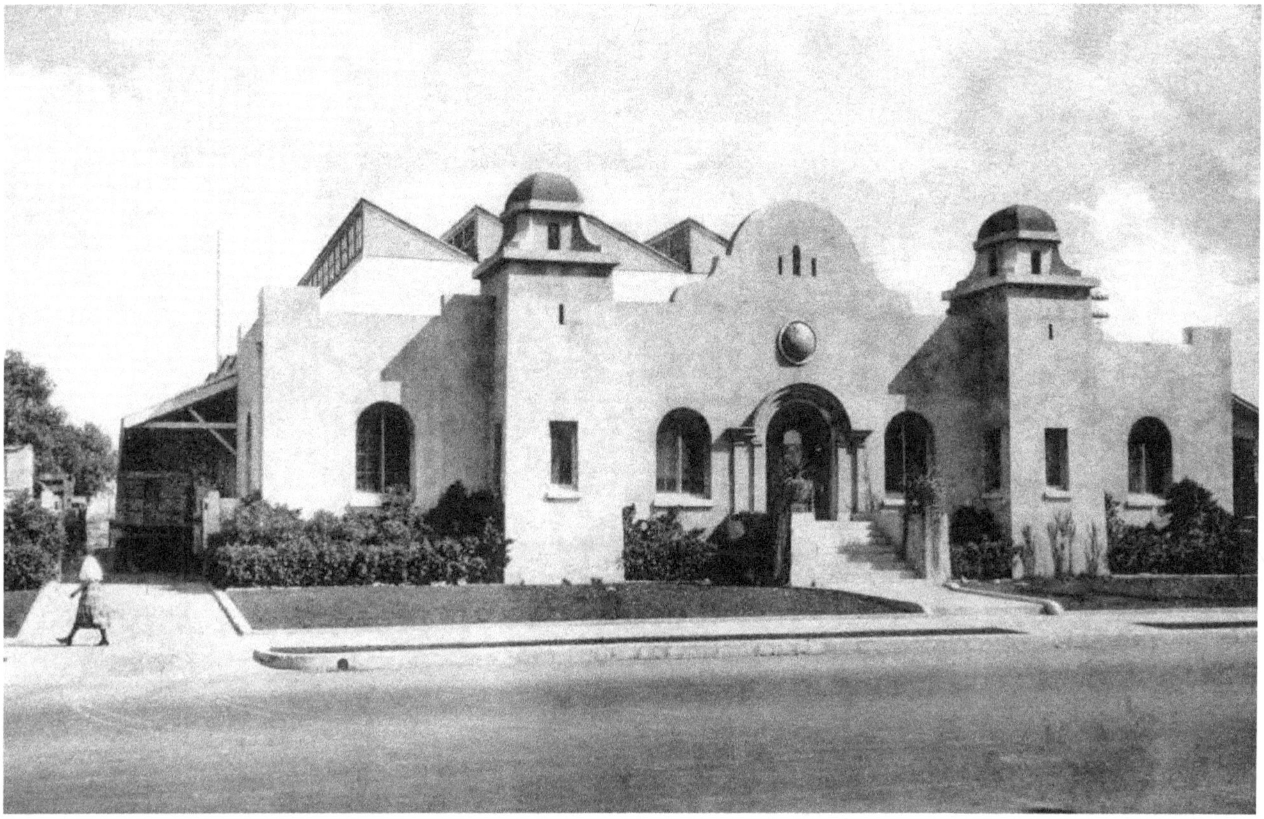

GRAND OPENING OF ANAHEIM PACKING HOUSE MAY 31

MY CONNECTIONS: FASHION, DIET , PLACES, AND SOCIAL TRENDS.....

INSIDE. DINING TIP INSIDE 10 BEST SOUTHERN CALIFORNIA RESATAURANT.

MY CONNECTIONS MAGAZINE

SPRING 2014

We try to reach the heart of Southern California readers by providing easy to read, short articles, and comprehensive know;ledge of the press release, post, articles, and images. We are about communication and show time in print or online, My Connections Magazine is celebrating one year birthday, and as we age together we expect much higher standards in everything we do. {The Editing Team}

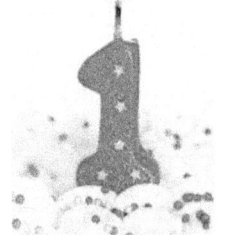

HAPPY ONE YEAR BIRTHDAY FOR MY CONNECTIONS MAGAZINE FROM ALL OF US {TET}.

www.ingramcontent.com/pod-product-compliance
Lightning Source LLC
Chambersburg PA
CBHW051949280526
45789CB00009B/3231